BRITAIN IN OLD PHOTOGRAPHS

AROUND THIRSK

*COOPER HARDING
AND PETER WYON*

SUTTON PUBLISHING

Sutton Publishing Limited · Phoenix Mill
Thrupp · Stroud · Gloucestershire · GL5 2BU

First Published in 1995

Reprinted in 2002

Copyright © Cooper Harding and Peter Wyon,
1995

A catalogue record for this book is available
from the British Library

ISBN 0 7509 0838 6

Typesetting and origination by
Sutton Publishing Limited.
Printed and bound in Great Britain by
J.H. Haynes & Co. Ltd, Sparkford.

No. 2 The Crescent. This fine Edwardian domestic exterior is part of the terrace seen in the photograph on p. 18. The identity of the girl in the doorway is not known, but she adds greatly to the charm of the picture.

Contents

Mr Ryder of Finkle Street, cycle and motor engineer in the early 1920s. This shop window still exists near the bridge at the foot of the street, though Ryder's has long departed. The casual stack of petrol cans typifies a less safety-conscious age. The pavement here is now edged with a line of bollards.

Introduction

Lying in the Vale of Mowbray between the scarp of the Hambleton Hills and the moorland of the Dales, Thirsk has long been the focus of trade for a score of villages. The earliest form of the name, Tresche, has a possible Celtic origin, denoting a settlement by a river; certainly the oldest dwellings cluster on either side of the Cod Beck.

On the east bank, St James' Green bears the name of a long-vanished chapel and was the traditional site for horse and cattle dealing. Across the bridge, the road leads into the Market Place proper, where the Market Cross and the Tolbooth once stood.

The Saxons were here; recent excavations on Castle Garth have uncovered some of their graves. The Normans built the castle, and the lands around became the fiefdom of Robert de Mowbray. The Mowbrays' castle was later destroyed, but by the fifteenth century the citizens of Thirsk were prosperous enough to undertake the complete rebuilding of their parish church.

Apart from the church, however, the architecture that we see today is largely the product of the eighteenth and nineteenth centuries, when the improvements made by the great landowners brought prosperity to the agricultural community. Surrounded by good grazing land, Thirsk was a market for sheep, cattle and horses. The Monday market and the annual fairs saw lively dealing in beasts and produce. Fellmongers and curriers traded in skins and hides, tanners, saddlers and shoemakers worked in the shops and sheds crammed into the yards behind the houses. There were corn mills and breweries. There was trade in wool and linen; the wool industry departed to the West Riding, but flax-dressing and linen-weaving remained local occupations until the middle 1800s; there was a dyer's establishment off Millgate and a drying-ground on the site of the present car park.

The town brought work for other craftsmen; there were blacksmiths and farriers, there was a small foundry in Norby, there were cartwrights, carpenters and joiners, tailors, haberdashers and the oldest draper's in the kingdom. Merchants and shopkeepers supplied the needs of town and country folk, while a score of taverns slaked their thirst.

The Quarter Sessions were convened at Thirsk where the local gentry sat as justices. The legal profession built prestigious town houses, or moved to the more salubrious surroundings of neighbouring Sowerby, where elegant Georgian villas mingle with humbler cottages along Front Street. Apothecaries, surgeons and physicians prospered and joined with the clergy, the wealthier farmers and successful merchants to form a social élite.

With the building of the turnpike roads, Thirsk became a post stage on the route from York to Edinburgh; three of the inns were noted as coaching establishments. Other houses offered stabling for horses that were the chief means of local transport until well into the present century.

The coming of the railway and, later, the growth of motor transport, combined with the effects of two world wars, brought radical changes to a way of life that had persisted for some two hundred years. Though the Market

Place is still busy on a Monday, the fairs have gone and there is no longer the teeming bustle remembered by older generations. Crafts have died out and family businesses have closed down, shops and pubs have vanished, feasts and sports are held no more.

The photographs collected here cover a period of nearly a hundred years, from the earliest examples taken in the 1870s to a few late pictures from the 1970s. The bulk of them are a visual record of the last part of the Victorian age, the brief but elegant reign of Edward VII, the grim years of the First World War and the more carefree days of the 1920s. They record scenes of an age that has passed, but which still lingers in the memories of the oldest living generation. The setting is often recognizable; Thirsk has grown well beyond its nineteenth-century boundaries, but the town has not suffered the wholesale demolitions that have swept away entire districts of larger urban areas. In the countryside the demands of road transport and the techniques of mechanical agriculture have transformed many aspects of the rural scene. The farming photographs convey that sense of community and companionship that marked a labour-intensive system where men and women, young and old, led a life that was often physically hard and poorly paid, but rarely lonely.

This period, before the arrival of the snapshot camera, was the heyday of the professional photographer and of the picture postcard. As well as urban views, country scenes and holiday souvenirs, postcards featured occasions that today would appear mainly in the press or on television – public and social events galore (every person in the crowd a likely customer!), while fires, floods and other disasters were popular subjects.

During this period, Thirsk was served by several photographers, of whom the finest was undoubtedly Joseph Robinson Clarke. Working from a studio by the bridge in Ingramgate, he had a wide clientele both in town and in the countryside. His formal shots are carefully composed, with the sharp detail characteristic of the slow emulsions of the day, but he had a ready eye for good business and seems to have been indefatigable in his attendance at public events of all kinds. His studio was strategically placed on the route into the town centre from the main York road. When the unusual passed his door, he was there to take the picture.

J.T. Fox ran a music store and also described himself as a news reporter. His name appears on a series of souvenir postcards of local views. Stevens & Co. were stationers, marketing their own range of cards.

W. Arthur Todd, from Carlton Husthwaite, took a number of photographs recording village scenes and events; these include a number of pictures taken in the fields probably for sale locally, but which have preserved views of farming activities not often seen.

Many of the photographs reproduced in this book come from the collection held by Thirsk Museum. The museum occupies an old house in Kirkgate which was the birthplace in 1755 of Thomas Lord, later to become the founder of the cricket ground in London which bears his name. The museum was founded in 1975 to preserve items representing the life and times of bygone generations from Thirsk and district. Many of those whose way of life is thus recorded appear in the photographs we have selected here.

THE TOWN

The Market Place, Thirsk, on a Monday in the late 1890s. The view is from Central Buildings towards Finkle Street, but the Dutch gables have not yet been added to the shops on the far side. The baskets in the foreground hold poultry and rabbits.

A rare view of the market from the east, late 1890s. The ancient Crown Inn with its low roof is in the centre on the far side. The shops on its left were later raised by two storeys, but the inn itself was demolished in 1968 to make way for a supermarket.

The north-east corner of the market seen about the same time. In the background to the left is the White Swan, now a hardware store.

Old shops, *c.* 1905. A horse collar hanging from a bracket distinguishes the premises of W. Scott, saddler. The firm is still in business in the Market Place today, but these shops were demolished in 1908 to make way for a new post office. The buildings here were an ancient encroachment on the open square; early drawings show them with low eaves and thatched roofs, already dilapidated in 1808 and condemned as 'rubbish' by a travelling writer. By the time the new electric lighting standard was installed in 1904, the shops had been re-roofed and smartened up. The cobbles of the Market Place have survived modern attempts to replace them with asphalt; this was the spot where in bygone times a cruel market by-law decreed the baiting of bulls sold for slaughter. A circle of cobbles is still marked out, with an iron ring at its centre. The wheeled contraption on the left was used to store the market trestles.

The Market Clock, early 1900s. This was erected in 1896 to commemorate the wedding three years earlier of the Duke of York (the future King George V) and Princess May of Teck. It stands on the site of the ancient Market Cross and originally housed a drinking fountain. It soon became the focus of activity in the town centre and is Thirsk's most well-known landmark.

Market day, 1920s. Motor transport was becoming more important in the years following the First World War, and market carts were giving way to vans and lorries. By this time the clock tower had lost its original gabled pinnacle, though the precise date of its disappearance is not recorded.

Westgate, early 1900s. As is the case throughout the north-east of England, 'gate' means 'street' and reflects the Scandinavian influence on place-names in the region. Just visible on the right is the police station, dating from 1854; the court house was added alongside in 1885. The present Town Hall had not yet been built, but the building beyond the trees was the Institute, providing a library and a large lecture room. The old Savings Bank stands at the end of Westgate; this, too, had a large assembly room on the first floor, now a physical fitness centre. There are two of Thirsk's many inns on the left-hand side of the street, the New Inn nearest the camera and the little Star beyond. The cyclists clearly had no need then to keep to the left on what is now a very busy road!

A view towards Castlegate, *c.* 1900. The ironmonger's (now the National Westminster Bank) stands on the site of Baker's drapery, destroyed by fire in 1864. The son of this old Quaker family, John Gilbert Baker, became a noted botanist at Kew, and was Keeper of the Herbarium from 1890 to 1899.

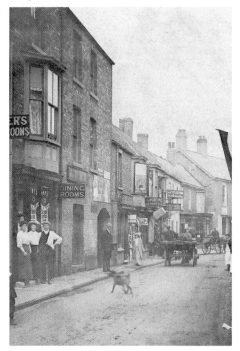

An informal view of Finkle Street, early 1900s. Narrow and curving, this is the only access to the Market Place from Ingramgate and York bridge, creating problems for modern traffic, but an effective defence in medieval times. On the left are Mrs Horner's Dining Rooms, with a newsagent's, sweet shop and shoe shop before coming to the Old Three Tuns where the street turns to the right.

Kirkgate, 1920s. Rhodes the brewer built the house on the right. Beyond is the Friends' Meeting House, established here in the seventeenth century. The car stands outside a doctor's premises. Co-author Peter Wyon lived here when he came to the town in 1939. It became a vet's surgery, made famous by the late Alf Wight, known to the world as James Herriot.

Looking down Kirkgate, August 1932. The Cross Keys is a very old house; the sign often marks a former ecclesiastical hostelry. The roof was once thatched, while the base of a timber 'cruck' in the end wall is a vestige of an early building technique. Mrs Barley stands in the gateway; she sold milk from cows that were kept in the yard behind the houses.

The Parish Church of St Mary the Virgin is a magnificent creation of the fifteenth century, with fretted parapets and a chancel built out over a vaulted crypt. St Mary's is seen here in Edwardian days, mirrored in the water of the dam that once supplied the town mill in Millgate. Between the mill dam and the Cod Beck was a grassy walk shaded by pollarded willows that once served to provide withies for basket-making. When the mill itself closed down the dam was no longer maintained, and was eventually filled in with rubble when the old cottages in Norby were pulled down in 1957. The whole area of the Holmes has been grassed over, and together with much of the old willow garth is happily preserved as a pleasant open space on the banks of the Beck.

William Dale Bateman, grocer, verger and parish clerk, was a highly respected figure in late Victorian Thirsk. He stands by the great south door of St Mary's with its original fifteenth-century tracery and massive lock. The parish chest is of ancient work, secured by three padlocks, the keys to which would have been held by the two churchwardens and the vicar respectively.

Outside the church, three anonymous craftsmen find a novel way to display these grotesque heads removed from the roof while repairs to the woodwork are carried out during the 1950s. With a number of vigorously decorated bosses and brackets, the carved timbers of the medieval roof are one of the glories of St Mary's.

Cemetery Lane runs between the church and the grounds of Thirsk Hall. The iron railings round the churchyard wall were removed to feed the steelworks during the Second World War. The smart carriage driven by a coachman in livery is approaching the vicarage; the workman with the cart stands aside, while a child from the hall cottages on the right watches from the gateway. The photograph probably dates from the 1890s.

The weir at Norby, *c.* 1900. The sluice at Norby controlled the flow of water to the town mill. The weir with its iron footbridge was a favourite viewpoint, though it was dangerous for children when the beck was in flood. The cottages, facing south, were part of Sunny Terrace; with the rest of old Norby, they were demolished in 1957 to make way for modern council homes.

A cattle market on St James' Green, *c*. 1907. There was a long tradition of cattle-dealing here. The building with the thatched cat-slide roof was the old Dolphin and Anchor inn. Electric lighting arrived in 1904, but the old gas lamps remained until the First World War.

A horse-dealer on the Green, *c*. 1904. Thirsk was renowned for its horses; local dealers supplied draught horses to many city employers and to the army. A number of houses on the Green had protective shutters fitted to ground-floor windows for use when markets were in progress.

The Methodist Chapel and School, *c.* 1910. John Wesley first preached in Thirsk in 1747 and a chapel was built on the Green in 1766, succeeded in 1816 by the building in the background. The big schoolroom dates from 1908 and was converted into a chapel to replace the nineteenth-century one, which was demolished in the 1960s.

The Crescent, 1970. Erected around 1890 by Manfield, the leading Thirsk builder, this elegant terrace with its private gardens fronting on the Cod Beck quickly became a very desirable address and many prominent families had their home here. A plan to build a similar terrace on the opposite side of Ingramgate was never realized.

Waterside, 1979. Thirsk has occasionally suffered spectacular flooding. A flood in July 1930 reached St James' Green and barrels floated down Finkle Street. These cottages were pulled down in 1992 and modern flats now stand on the site.

Washing sheep in the Beck. This is perhaps the oldest photograph in the collection, probably dating from the 1870s. Sheep are being dipped in the Cod Beck from a field known as Green Garth, which lay beyond the cottages seen in the photograph above, later occupied by Todd's builders' yard.

The last days of Rymer's mill. This large eighteenth-century town mill had steam power added in 1855, having fulled cloth, milled snuff and briefly driven cotton-spinning machinery in the late 1700s. It ceased working in the 1950s, and stood derelict until it was finally demolished in the early '70s.

After the demolition of the mill, the foundations were laid out as a riverside garden, seen here under water during the 1979 flood. The extensive bakery buildings shown in the photograph have now been converted into housing.

TRADE AND INDUSTRY

*In the 1920s and '30s this was Maxwell's shoe
shop, formerly W. Allanson's. Tucked in a corner
of the Market Place next to the Golden Lion,
this was a high-class shop, Mr Maxwell himself
being 'well-spoken and a gentleman'. A Chinese
restaurant now occupies this site.*

Harker's wheelwright's shop in Long Street, 1920s. This was an old-established family business, combining undertaking with joinery. From left to right: Alf Horner, apprentice, Teesdale Bagley, joiner, Wilf Bell, joiner, George Harker himself, and Fred Hammond, wheelwright. The display outside the workshop shows that kennels, coops and hutches were also part of the firm's stock-in-trade. Both workshop and house look very trim. The tree trained on the front of the house was once a familiar sight in the town, noted particularly in former days for its apricots. Plums and pears were also grown in this fashion, though few survive today. The house is now Swift's, plumber and heating engineer, while the adjoining workshop is a fish and chip shop.

Amos Dixon, bootmaker and repairer, moved from his premises shown here to a single-storey shop at the top of the Market Place, where his son Bertie later practised as a chiropodist and which is now Cottage Antiques. A ladies' fashion shop now occupies the premises with the Market Pharmacy to the right.

George Ayre and Son, grocer's and chemist's. This shop had just been modernized by the addition of the Dutch gables when this photograph was taken; the façade bears a terracotta plaque inscribed 'A 1901'. On the corner of Finkle Street, the premises were well sited; later Rukin's shoe shop, they now house car accessories.

A fine example of an Edwardian shopfront. Robson and Ingham had only a short tenure here before being succeeded by Willie Clayton. This shop survived till the late 1940s.

Masterman's shop next to Hall's Fleece Hotel, as it was in about 1910. The gateway was the old coach entrance to the inn yard. The yards round the Market Place housed numerous businesses of all kinds; Henry Masterman's wine and spirit stores can be seen beyond the gateway. The shop is now occupied by a building society.

B. Smith & Sons, *c*. 1890. This firm claimed to have been trading in Thirsk since 1580, and with nearly four centuries behind it, it merited an entry in the *Guinness Book of Records*. Bartholomew Smith (1830–1912) was a local artist who seems to have been happy to leave the running of the shop to his business-like Quaker son-in-law. Girls lived on the premises to be trained as sempstresses, a much sought-after qualification. The grocery department was sold off in 1952; the draper's continued into the next decade, but finally ceased trading, whereupon the premises became one of the few Market Place buildings to be demolished in the 1970s.

Foggitt's chemist's, *c.* 1905. The photograph shows a typical old-fashioned chemist's window with its customary coloured bottles, now succeeded by Boots. One of Thirsk's leading citizens, William Foggitt was a fervent Methodist and a noted naturalist. The name is best known today as that of Thirsk's highly individual weather expert.

Kerbside petrol pumps, 1960s. Now trading as Woodhead and Bray, the motor distribution firm occupied this site for several years before moving to its present premises on Station Road. The array of pumps was typical of the period.

The Lambert Memorial Hospital, 1890. Founded by Mrs Sarah Lambert in memory of her husband and her father-in-law, both surgeons, the little hospital was built on Chapel Street with a view over the Flatts.

In the early 1900s Mr Harry Tibbits, LDS, had his surgery above Masterman's wine store next to the Fleece. He advertised sets of teeth from £2 2s and painless extractions 'by the American Method'.

The new post office and staff, 1909. The earlier post office was on the north side of the Market Place. This grand new building replaced the old shops seen in the photograph on p. 9. The door on the far right was the entrance to the public section of the office; at the rear was a sorting office and yard, in the middle of which stood the poles carrying telephone wires to the premises round the Market Place. The parade of staff is impressive, as are the smart delivery carts that served outlying villages. The telegram boys were familiar figures in the days before telephones in the home, though their arrival often meant bad news. The building has now been converted into shop units, though the foundation stone carrying the date 1909 has been preserved.

James Biltcliffe, confectioner and pastry-cook, *c.* 1905. His shop was on the corner of Castlegate and Westgate, with windows displaying a fine selection of goods. He advertised 'First-class Fare at Moderate Charges' and offered 'Home-made Bread and Tea-cakes fresh daily'.

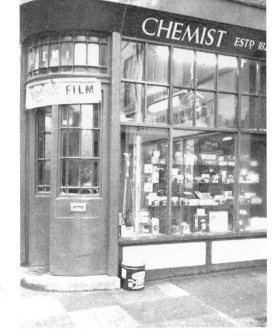

The doors to the Market Pharmacy, 1970s. Originally Knagg's, this shop has been a chemist's for a century or more, though it has changed owner several times. The double doors on the corner are much older than the shop front; the curved style suggests Georgian origins.

Another of Thirsk's old businesses. The Johnsons lived on the premises. The gateway on the right leads into Johnson's Yard, a picturesque corner of the town still in active use. Wooden setts remain in the entrance, designed to deaden the rumble of carts passing the living quarters.

Rhodes' brewery in Kirkgate was taken over by John Smith's of Tadcaster in 1897, after which it was used simply for storage and distribution. It later became a builder's yard, but was eventually converted into flats. The old brewery chimney remains, the last to survive in the town.

The Queen's Head Inn, *c.* 1910. This inn is typical of many small beer houses in the district, consisting usually of one small bar parlour with the back room serving as a cellar. Situated in Barbeck, this pub was popularly known as the Ramping Cat, an uncomplimentary reference to the Queen in question. Landlord William Harland stands in front of the door.

Adam Carlisle Bamlett, 1878. Bamlett brought agricultural engineering to Thirsk in 1860 when, aged twenty-six, he built his works in Station Road. He successfully pioneered mechanical grass-cutters and his machines won a world-wide reputation. He died in 1912; there is a mosaic tablet to his memory in Sowerby Church.

Workmen at Bamlett's, *c.* 1895. The works in Station Road included a large timber yard employing steam-driven pit saws. Among these workmen is John Norris, third from the right, seen in uniform on p. 105.

Bamlett's single-shafted sheafer, 1880. Before the reaper-binder had been perfected, the single shaft enabled this sheafing machine to be drawn by a horse walking clear of the mown corn.

The self-propelled cutter, *c*. 1920. Nicknamed 'Percy', this prototype machine was an attempt to apply early tractor technology to the cutter, but it never went into production.

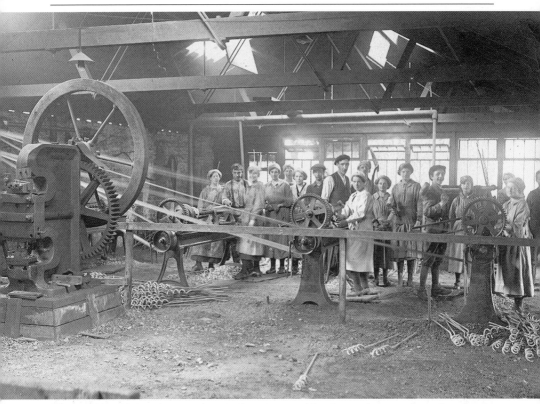

The machine shop, *c.* 1916. During the First World War Bamlett's undertook a certain amount of war production, notably gun-carriage parts and screw-posts for supporting barbed wire. All over the country women replaced the men who had joined up, and the work-force in this photograph is largely female. The machines used to form the screw-posts piled on the floor are all belt-powered, running from line-shafting on the left of the shop.

Lathe operators, early 1900s. A typical machine shop scene. As in the photograph on the opposite page, the machines are all belt-powered.

The latter years at Bamlett's. Eric Abbott with Mrs Thackrah at a milling machine, c. 1970. After the Second World War the firm retained some women employees. The machine here is electrically driven.

The old goods yard and Bamlett's seen from Station Road, 1975. A victim of the recession of the 1980s, the firm went into receivership in 1986, was sold up and the works demolished. A supermarket and car park now occupy this site.

Thirsk Power House, 1929. This photograph of the power house in Station Road is signed by H.D. Phelps, the engineer designer. Gas was in use in Thirsk from 1836; electricity came in 1904. This installation marks the change to diesel-driven generators.

Section Three

EVENTS AND
OCCASIONS

*Military Sunday, 1913. The parade is drawn up
outside what is now the Midland Bank, with the
Girl Guide contingent in a prominent position.*

Thirsk Parish Church Choir, 1887. Forty-five men and boys appear in this group, together with the vicar, curate and organist; few cathedrals could muster that number today. Tallest in the back row to the right of centre is Reginald Bell, Lord of the Manor and Squire of Thirsk. Second from the left in the front row is Zaccheus (Zack) Wright, stationer, printer and noted sportsman. The vicar in 1887 was Right Revd C.E. Cambidge, Lord Bishop of Bathurst. His curate, Revd Eusebius Richardson, had a talent for amateur theatre. The organist was T.H. Fall. Note the hobnailed soles displayed by the two young choirboys on the right.

Thirsk Market Place, Coronation Day, 9 August 1902. This photograph, featured on the cover of the book, was taken at 3.20 p.m. when the official festivities in the Market Place were over, but a few lingering youngsters were still in best bib and tucker and ready to wave a flag. There is much to be seen in this picture, which merits careful study. The cobbles, as always, were causing problems; the two paviours in the middle distance have left their barrow, tools and pile of stones to watch the photographer.

Coronation celebrations in Sowerby, 1902. In the grounds of Manor Farm the childrens' treat under the awnings is in full swing. This photograph and the two following were taken by A.C. Bamlett.

A pause for conversation as the coronation festivities proceed. This photograph offers some fine fashion studies.

An interesting contrast with the previous photograph. Behind the scenes, the village ladies are seen washing up. They are looking over the wall into Front Street.

Flower Show, 1910. Although this photograph is dated, there is no indication of where the show is taking place, though it could be in the grounds of Thirsk Hall. The table display on the right shows a model cottage.

Thirsk Fire Brigade, early 1900s. The engine-shed still stands at the end of the Three Tuns yard. In 1918 it took so long to catch the horse grazing on the Flatts that Upsall Castle was burnt down before the engine arrived!

Soldiers watering horses in the Cod Beck, 1906. Cavalry units were regular visitors to Thirsk in the 1900s. Horses bred here were in great demand as army mounts.

Gypsies on the move, Westgate, 1906. Quite a crowd has gathered to watch these tented carts make their way through the town. The gypsies may well have been on their way to Topcliffe Fair, a noted rendezvous which took place in July. Local belief is that these were German gypsies; it is perhaps more likely that they were from Hungary or elsewhere in Eastern Europe. It is worth comparing this picture with the one on p. 11; the court house can be seen next to the police station on the right. The open space behind the trees was later to be the site of the Town Hall.

A Methodist convention at Thirsk. The date of this photograph is not known, but these Methodist ministers are dressed in the style of the late 1800s. They are grouped in Castle Garth; Castle Villa, seen in the top right-hand corner, had recently been built by the Johnson family and they may have been hosting this gathering. The rising ground against which the group is posed is the remains of the mound on which Thirsk Castle was built in Norman times. Excavations near this spot in 1994 revealed several Saxon burials, suggesting that this site could well pre-date the Conquest.

General Booth drives through Thirsk, 1908. William Booth was himself a Methodist minister before founding the Salvation Army in 1878. The eighty-year-old General is greeting the crowd in Long Street at the corner of Ingramgate.

Quarter Master Sergt. J. Walker,
WESTMORLAND HOUSE, THIRSK.

THE POPULAR THIRSK EVANGELIST AND VOCALIST had the honour to Sing before Her Late Majesty, Queen Victoria, and Members of the Royal Family, Parkhurst, I. O. W., 1884; also received the thanks of Her Late Majesty, Queen Victoria, for his Diamond Jubilee Hymn. Known as the Soldier Poet.

QSM J. Walker, evangelist and vocalist, *c*. 1905. We have not so far traced Sergeant Walker's career, but his name appears as a regular performer at Saturday evening entertainments in the 1890s. His repertoire included both the serious and the sentimental, even the comic solo, 'Oh, Mr Porter!'.

A watering party in Barbeck, 1908. Training camps for the Volunteers were annual events in Thirsk. A young NCO is in charge of a party filling the water-cart from a standpipe. The ancient thatched cottage beyond has given way to a garage.

1st Thirsk Scouts, 1909. *Scouting for Boys* was published in 1908 and the Scout movement became instantly popular. This was the first troop to be formed in Thirsk.

General Election, 1910. Lord Helmsley, returned with a majority of 1,185, acknowledges the cheers of the crowd from a window in the assembly room above the Savings Bank in Castlegate.

The Thirsk Suffragette. No further information is given on this card, which must date from roughly the same time as the election recorded above. The background suggests that the fête was taking place in one of the hillside villages.

Coronation celebrations, 1911. The Scout bugle band provides a fanfare to mark the coronation of George V. The crowd is gathered outside the Fleece Hotel, run by the Hall family for nearly a century. Note that by 1911 the inn was offering garaging as well as post horses.

Parish Church Schools Festival, 1912. This was an annual event, with a church service, a parade with decorated floats, singing in the Market Place, tea on the Green and sports in the grounds of Thirsk Hall. The gentleman holding the straw hat is leading the singing in front of the new post office.

The funeral of Sir George Wombwell, 1913. Sir George Orby Wombwell owned the Newburgh Priory estate at Coxwold. He was a survivor of the Charge of the Light Brigade at Balaclava in 1854. With his wife, Lady Julia, he was a much-loved figure. Here the hearse is about to pass the Fauconberg Arms on its way to Coxwold church.

Military Sunday, 1912. Parades of uniformed organizations were a feature of the public calendar in the years leading up to the First World War. Girl Guides and Red Cross units are drawn up in the Market Place. There is a good view of the old Crown between the shops on the far side.

Military Sunday, 1914. On the eve of the First World War, a parade of uniformed organizations marches down Ingramgate towards the Market Place. The women in the foremost unit are nurses of the Voluntary Aid Detachment.

Women's VAD display, 1914. Thirsk Voluntary Aid Detachment produced the winning team. Within a few weeks these nurses were facing a much more serious challenge as Britain went to war.

Sandhutton National Rifle Volunteer Reserves, 1916. Two veterans of the South African war proudly wear their old uniforms in this home front defence unit, forerunner of the 1940s Home Guard.

St Oswald's Church Lads' Brigade, 1915. The CLB was founded in 1891 as a Christian youth movement, aiming to teach boys discipline through pride in uniform and regular drill. The rifles would seem out of place today.

Four Thirsk nurses, *c.* 1917. On the left is Miss Edith Johnson; she went on to have a long career in local nursing. Her friends are, left to right: Mrs Holliday, Miss Moss (later Mrs Bulmer) and Miss M. Jackson.

Thirsk men's ambulance unit. First on the left in the front row is Walter Power, who appears in a very different role on p. 122.

Thirsk War Play, 1915. Britannia and John Bull join hands in a tableau from this patriotic community production.

This group is simply headed 'Britain'. Earlier scenes included one portraying the plight of Belgian refugees. We do not know if a script for this play has survived.

The convalescent hospital in Thirsk Town Hall, 1914. The Town Hall was opened in 1913. Once the war began, it was converted into a hospital for wounded servicemen, with volunteer VAD nurses. In this early photograph the stage scenery has not yet been removed.

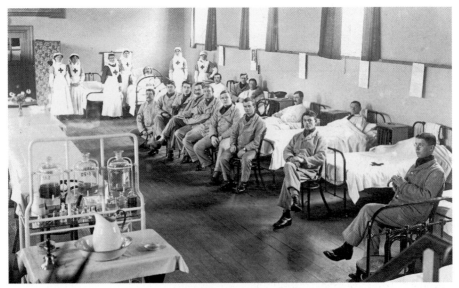

The hospital, 1915. The ward is now properly organized, the men wearing the regulation 'hospital blue'. Clarke took group photographs of each batch of patients right through the war; they were popular souvenirs.

Corporal Lazenby, Christmas 1914. Clark took a large number of studio shots of servicemen as they went off to war; sometimes it was the last photograph ever taken of the men.

Private Harry Bulmer, 28 December 1914. Harry Bulmer survived the war; he was later noted as a keen sportsman and hockey umpire.

Convalescent Tommies, Westgate, 1916. The wagonette may have been about to take the soldiers to the station. Lambert's fish shop was opposite the Town Hall; earlier it had been the Star public house.

Private J. Daglish and family, *c*. 1916. Though the family is putting on a brave face here, this photograph is somehow more convincing than the posed studio portraits on the previous page.

Sergeant Will Stephenson, 1918. 'Oh no, he has not got me yet!' was the message sent home on this postcard from the Italian front. Will Stephenson, first on the left, was wounded soon after and later died when his hospital was bombed. He had been a builder in civilian life; the girls had called him 'Bonnie Brickie'.

'Après la guerre finie.' Dated 1919, this must have been one of the last photographs taken of a hospital group. Edith Johnson and her fellow nurses can be recognized from the photograph on p. 52.

Victory Parade, 1919. Though the Armistice was signed on 11 November 1918, peace was not celebrated till the following year. The procession is making its way towards the platform ready for the judging of the costumes and tableaux.

Presenting the prizes. Captain Reginald Bell, seated in uniform on the platform, looks on as his wife presents first prize. The platform stands in front of Jordison's dining rooms, still a popular café today.

Silver Jubilee party on St James' Green, 1935. The twenty-first anniversary of the accession of George V was celebrated in grand style. The royal souvenir mugs on the tables were presented to the children on this occasion; many of those mugs still survive today.

Gas-mask drill at Topcliffe, 1939. The war clouds gather again as Mr W.G. Burton, headmaster, instructs his pupils in donning their civilian respirators. The cardboard cases slung on a string were the standard issue.

Prisoner-of-war camp, 1944. This hutted camp on the Stockton Road was built to house Italian prisoners engaged on agricultural work. After the war the huts were improved to provide temporary civilian housing.

Fire at Gilling's Sowerby works, 1948. This old-established leather factory was totally destroyed in this blaze, but was rebuilt and operated until 1993. The firemen are wearing wartime steel helmets.

TRANSPORT

*A horse bus in Ingramgate, c. 1900. The railway
arrived in 1841, but horse-drawn transport was
the usual means of conveyance locally for the best
part of a century to come.*

Railway disaster at Thirsk, 2 November 1892. In the early hours of the foggy morning of 2 November 1892 the Edinburgh to London express ploughed into the rear of a goods train at Manor House junction, not far from Thirsk. The collision was the result of a signalling error, but the horror of the crash was increased by fire breaking out in the wreckage before all the victims could be pulled clear. In all ten passengers died and thirty-nine were injured. The death of five-year-old Lottie Hamilton caused particular emotion locally, and a stone to her memory can be seen in the cemetery, erected by the children of Thirsk.

Thirsk station, early 1900s. Until recent times, Thirsk was an important interchange point on the old LNER. The station had noted refreshment rooms on both platforms and a large staff. Well-known faces were often to be spotted among the passengers changing for Leeds or the North.

Thirsk station platform staff, 1915. There are nineteen men in this photograph, a measure both of the level of staffing and of the importance of this station in the early years of the century.

Picking up mail at speed. This pick-up point was on the main line, south of Thirsk station. Mail-bags were hung from the arm to be caught up by a rack extended from the postal van of the express passing at full speed. Letters were then sorted en route. A bag of incoming mail can be seen as a blur in the net beneath.

Pony and trap, 1920s. For many farming families this was the easiest means of getting to town and back.

Hall's station bus, *c.* 1900. The Fleece Hotel ran its own horse bus to convey customers to and from the station. It advertised 'All trains met'.

A motor charabanc, *c.* 1912. This magnificent vehicle with its tiered rows of seats replaced the horse bus in the early years of the century.

An NER motor bus, *c.* 1918. The station bus service was taken over by the North Eastern Railway who ran this vehicle, an improvement on the open charabanc. The crew are Joe and Arthur Stephenson.

Spot the differences! There are enough to suggest that this is a new improved model of the bus above. Both photographs are taken outside Clarke's studio in Ingramgate. Ingram House forms the background; it was owned by Lady Frankland and had extensive gardens until The Crescent was built in its grounds.

Motoring at Birdforth. There is no further information about this photograph, but it is most evocative of the early days of the automobile. The car is probably driving along the main Thirsk to York road – the modern A19!

A motor smash at Birdforth. We hope this is not the same vehicle as that shown above, but again we know nothing more about this photograph. The car seems well and truly ditched.

Nurses at the Town Hall hospital, 1918. The period details of this large car are well displayed. It seems as though the young ladies are simply posing for the camera, since there is still a rug covering the radiator.

Donnie Stevens at Beech House, Carlton Husthwaite, with a Raleigh motor cycle decorated for a show. The motor cycle was very much a development of the 1920s and local contests were popular – see p. 116.

AROUND THE VILLAGES

Distant view of Thirsk from Plump Bank in the early years of the century. This is the eastern approach to the town from Sutton Bank. The road is now wider and straighter, but the view remains.

The Old Manor House, Sowerby, early 1900s. Sowerby is Thirsk's nearest neighbour, but still preserves a distinct identity. The house on the left has a long history, owned first by the Lascelles and then by the Bells, who became Lords of Thirsk Manor in 1722. Nearly derelict by 1990, it has now been restored.

Front Street, Sowerby, at about the same period as above. A number of fine Georgian houses line the broad main street of the village. The open grass verges were planted with rows of lime trees in 1887 to mark the Golden Jubilee of Queen Victoria's reign.

Sowerby Methodist Chapel, built 1865. This view looks north up Front Street. The lime trees are again in evidence. This photograph dates from about 1900.

Sowerby Grange, early 1900s. This spacious Victorian house with its ample lawns is typical of the residences of the wealthier citizens. For a while it was the home of George Freeman – see p. 110.

Victory Row at the turn of the century. This terrace was built by Sir Ralph Payne-Gallwey and named after his party had won an election. It was also known as 'Blue Row' and more irreverently as 'Bribery Terrace'. Note the presence of two postmen.

Lock Bridge, 1890s. In 1768 work began on a canal to link Thirsk with the Swale. A wharf was built in the town, with a lock on the Cod Beck in Sowerby, but the promoters ran out of funds and work came to an end. A bridge was built with the massive stones prepared for the lock.

Griffin Farm, Bagby. This fine farmhouse on the York to Thirsk road was once the Griffin Inn, serving coaches on the shorter runs. The yard is still open to the highway.

The Old Sycamore Tree, *c.* 1900. This ancient tree was long famous as the largest standing 'between hedges' on any road between London and Edinburgh. Age claimed it in the 1940s, though the site was still marked on the OS map of 1950.

St Mary's Church, Bagby, *c.* 1890. Bagby is one of the earliest recorded parishes in the district, but this church, of a most unusual design, replaced a much older building in 1862.

Bagby village, *c.* 1900. With its long single street winding its way up from the York road, Bagby preserves much ancient charm. Some of its cottages are very old.

Bagby School, 1931. This photograph will bring back memories for some of Bagby's residents today. These little village schools were at the heart of the community. The school itself is now closed, but the building serves as the church hall.

Miss Mary Booth, headmistress of Bagby school. The photograph was taken in the 1920s when Miss Booth had retired after forty-five years service in Bagby. She was a much-loved figure for three generations of villagers.

Great Thirkleby in the early years of the century. This part of Thirkleby was an 'estate' village, forming part of the Frankland properties. On the other side of the beck, Little Thirkleby was part of Lord Downe's estate. Both were sold up after the First World War.

Thirkleby Hall, c. 1900. This fine mansion was completed in 1785 for Sir Thomas Frankland to designs by James Wyatt. The estate passed to the Payne-Gallwey family, but was sold up in the 1920s. The mansion itself was demolished in 1927; only the lodge gates and the stable block remain.

Capt. William Thomas Payne-Gallwey. Serving with the Grenadier Guards, this veteran of the Boer War was lost in action on the Western Front in 1914. He was the only son of Sir Ralph Payne-Gallwey, who himself died in 1916, the estate being left without a direct heir.

The Fauconberg Arms, Coxwold, 1890s. Newburgh Priory was the home of the Bellasis family, Lords Fauconberg. This old inn, thatched at one time, is shown with a fine signboard bearing the family arms. It is still a popular hostelry.

The Black Bull, Husthwaite. This rare half-timbered house overlooking the tiny village green in Husthwaite was still an inn when this photograph was taken. It is now a private residence.

Kilburn School, 1940. The children of the village school are grouped by the church gate. The village schools taught the whole age-range of children; few would go on to secondary education in those days.

Kilburn, 1904. The white horse on the hillside above the village was carved out by the men of Kilburn in 1857 to the design of John Hodgson, the schoolmaster. It measures 314 ft in length, is 228 ft high and is visible for miles across the Vale of Mowbray; not being on chalk like other hill figures, it requires periodic refurbishing. Kilburn is noted as the home of Robert Thompson, the joiner who took to signing his furniture with the figure of a church mouse. His pieces are greatly sought after, and known all over the world. The tradition he began is continued by craftsmen in modern workshops today.

The Hambleton Hotel, early 1900s. This inn was popular in the days before 1776 when races enjoying royal patronage were held here. With extensive stables, it retained importance as a training centre after the races moved to York. Note the cycles as well as the horse-drawn brake.

An iron ore mine at Kirby Knowle in the early twentieth century. The Hambleton Hills have been mined in the past for coal and iron. This drift mine was opened as a trial, but did not produce enough to be worth developing.

The crab-mill at Sutton-under-Whitestonecliffe, early 1900s. Sutton lies at the foot of the formidable Sutton Bank. This ancient village mill was used for crushing crab-apples to make cider-vinegar, known locally as 'verjuice'.

The gardens of Sutton Hall before the First World War. For many years Sutton Hall was the neglected home of an eccentric elderly lady, but it was bought in the early 1900s by Mr James Edwards. He refurbished the house and planted fine ornamental gardens, which are seen here in a typical Clarke photograph.

The Old Thatch, Carlton Husthwaite, 1920s. This fine example of a thatched timber-frame house is an unusual survivor in an area where most building is in local brick.

The garden of the Old Thatch. In recent years, a large modern extension has been added to the rear of this old house, which still has a large garden running out to the back lane.

The Manor House, Carlton Husthwaite, early 1920s. The photograph shows the house before the left-hand wing was raised to the same height as the gabled front. This was the home of W. Arthur Todd, who took a number of the photographs in this section and the next.

The Panelled Room at the Manor House. This is a very rare photograph of an interior remarkable for its painted panelling and the elegance of its furnishing.

The Old Hall, Carlton Husthwaite, in the first years of the century. The Old Hall is thought to have been built for a member of the Kitchingman family in the late seventeenth century. It is an impressive house, standing at the entrance to the village, and was home to four generations of the Ward family until 1954.

Carlton Church, early 1900s. The congregation are seen leaving the church at the end of the morning service. The church stands on the village green, where the horse-chestnut tree is now a mighty specimen.

Carlton Church, *c.* 1910. This church has a fine seventeenth-century interior. The pulpit bears the date 1678 and has a sounding board with an ornate canopy.

Carlton Methodist Chapel in a photograph taken at about the same time as the one above. This chapel was built alongside the church in 1869 at a cost of £200, raised by subscription. The adjoining building was the village reading room. Both have now been converted into private houses.

The Black Lion, Carlton, 1920s. Once the Carpenter's Arms and now the Carlton Inn this was a typical small village inn. Charles Newbald was the landlord here in the 1890s. The Old Hall can be seen at the bottom of the street.

Cyclists at Carlton, 1920s. 'Teas. Cyclists catered for' reads the notice by the door of the Black Lion. These cyclists certainly seem happy with the catering.

Birdforth Church at about the turn of the century. Birdforth is a tiny hamlet, but gives its name to the wapentake, the traditional administrative district which includes Thirsk. This little church has never had electric light installed; it is still used for services twice a year, at harvest and Christmas.

Birdforth School, 1920s. The headmaster was Mr D.L. Smith. The teacher on the left of the girls was Miss Baines, later to become Mrs Ball. The young lady behind her was Minnie Draper, a pupil-teacher. The school building is now The Gables restaurant.

The Busby Stoop Inn at the end of the nineteenth century. In the early eighteenth century a certain Thomas Busby was convicted of the murder of local farmer Daniel Auty, his father-in-law and confederate in a counterfeiting operation. After his execution, Busby's corpse was hung in irons from a gibbet erected at this lonely crossroads on the road to Northallerton, and the spot took its name from the post or 'stoop' which served as a grisly reminder of Busby's crime. This was reputed to be a haunted spot, and later superstitions centred on a particular armchair that stood in the bar parlour of this roadside inn. It is now to be seen in Thirsk Museum.

Sandhutton, early 1900s. This village stands less than a mile north of the Busby Stoop crossroads. This early photograph shows the village pump, and beyond it the smithy. The Reynolds, father and son, were blacksmiths and farriers here for the best part of a century.

Catton School, 1938. Catton is a tiny village lying on the River Swale to the west of Thirsk and Topcliffe. The young teacher in the centre of the back row seems scarcely old enough to have sole charge of the school.

Topcliffe, *c.* 1910. Once an important market town on the banks of the Swale and a stronghold of the powerful Percy family, Topcliffe later 'dwindled to the quietude of a rural village'. The remains of the cross show where the market-place used to be.

Dishforth, *c.* 1905. There is still an airfield here, dating from the days of the Second World War. This photograph shows the main street in more peaceful days. Dixon's mobile boot repair service has travelled out from Thirsk; the same van appears in the picture on p. 23.

Revd Henry Hawkins, Vicar of Topcliffe, 1885. 'A large-hearted Christian and benevolent to the poor', the gentle cleric who forms the subject of this noted portrait by J.R. Clarke was vicar of St Columba's, Topcliffe, for fifty-three years until his death at the age of 78 in 1891.

Topcliffe Fair, 1904. Gallopers, a showman's engine, booths and caravans all go to make up a fine picture of the traditional fairground.

Gypsies at Topcliffe in the early part of the century. 'Topley' Fair was held in mid-July; a traditional rendezvous for gypsies, tinkers and horse-copers from far and near, it had a bad reputation for rowdiness. By the 1960s pressure was growing to bring it to an end and the fair was held for the last time in 1969.

FAMILY AND FARMING LIFE

*Joseph Smithson, taking a leisurely pipe by the
summerhouse in the garden at The Cedars,
c. 1920. He was a prosperous farmer and
potato merchant.*

Leading timber near Kepwick, *c.* 1900. This fine photograph of horses drawing a timber rig is thought to have been taken on the Over Silton to Nether Silton road, with the turn to Kepwick on the right. With the horses walking in single file and the wheels of the rig on independent axles, loads of timber were remarkably manoeuvrable on narrow tracks.

Newly clipped! Harry Smithson is seen with Strawberry at the Cedars, Carlton Husthwaite, *c.* 1910.

Betty and Blossom, early 1920s. Tom Marwood with the horses at the Old Hall, Carlton. He is wearing an old army tunic; discarded service clothing has always proved useful working dress.

The miller's wagon, 1890. Rymer's wagoner Mr Watson poses for the camera while his team of three feed from their nosebags. The stout build of the wagon was needed to cope with the weight of grain or flour that was carried.

Drilling seed. This large implement with its team of men, horses and following harrow seems cumbersome compared with modern tractor-drawn machines.

Potato pickers at Carlton Husthwaite. Posing at 'drinkings' time, Charlotte Slater, Bessie Smithson, Polly Marwood and Jane Thompson (standing left to right) share a laborious job here with the men and boys. The wet mud on their sacking aprons gives some idea of the damp and cold endured in the fields, but it was a welcome chance to earn extra cash. Schools in Thirsk had a fortnight's potato-picking holiday in October, which survives today as the autumn half-term break.

Cattle beet. There seems here to be a good crop of this essential winter feed for cattle. Harvesting beet was another heavy job, while topping and tailing the roots ready for storage called for both skill and a strong wrist.

Lowance time, 1920s. These haymakers have already piked a fair quantity of hay and are taking their break for food, the time 'allowed' by custom. Note the basket and the standard 'lowance cans'.

The reaper-binder, *c.* 1920. The clatter of the mechanical reaper at work in the harvest field was one of the familiar sounds of high summer in the countryside and could be heard as late as the 1950s.

Harvest time, 1920s. Harry Stevens, centre, may have something stronger than cold tea in the stone jar; harvesting was thirsty work. The lads have their sticks ready to chase and despatch any rabbits breaking cover from the shrinking belt of uncut corn.

Corn ready for threshing, 1910. These trim ricks at Crowtrees Farm, Hutton Sessay, are the product of great skill both in stacking and in thatching. The threshing engine stands ready in the stackyard.

William Feather's prize sow, 1890s. This sow won first prize for the Feathers at the agricultural show; they were awarded a silver cruet.

The Feathers at West Farm, Islebeck, 1898. This photograph hung unidentified in Thirsk Museum until 1993, when it was recognized by a visitor from New Zealand as showing his grandmother's family on their farm near Thirsk. A copy of the picture had gone with the family to New Zealand in 1905. William Feather is holding the plough, while his son Jack holds the traces of the second pair of horses; the rest of his family and stock are dotted about the field.

The Feather family, grouped outside the farmhouse door, 1898. Back row, left to right: William jnr, Thomas Barker, Christiana, John Henry, Annie Elizabeth Victoria and Annie Mary Victoria. Front row: William Feather snr, Frank, Edith, Mary Elizabeth Caroline (née Crosby). The twins were born in Golden Jubilee year, 1887, which accounts for the addition of the name Victoria. Frank, the baby, is in petticoats; boys and girls were dressed alike when they were toddlers. The family emigrated to New Zealand in 1905, where William continued farming until his death in 1945 aged 93. He never lost his Yorkshire accent. Young Frank volunteered for the army in 1914, but died of pneumonia in Cairo on his way to Europe. Christiana married the same year; this Clarke photograph was sent to us by Christiana's grandson, Mike Connelly of Tauranga, North Island.

A birthday party at Carlton Husthwaite, 1906. Emma Smithson is celebrating her twenty-first birthday with her party guests at The Cedars. Emma is standing second from the left; her father, Joseph, wears a bowler hat, while her mother is sitting in front of him.

Dipping sheep, *c*. 1920. To keep dry, the man dipping the sheep sometimes stood in a barrel, but here John Marwood of Carlton Husthwaite looks as if he is getting very wet!

The family engine at the turn of the century. A traction-engine was an expensive item but a useful investment, since it could be hired out around the neighbourhood. The engine in this photograph is undergoing an overhaul, but the family pride is evident.

Myers' threshing set, 1895. This 1888 Marshall engine was owned by William Myers of Sandhutton. The driver is William jnr, and the steersman is Sam Bell. The regulation flagman walking ahead is John Seaton.

2509 Pte John Norris of the King's Own
Scottish Borderers, *c.* 1890. With his elder
brother Bill, John joined the 25th
Regiment of Foot in 1880 and served for
some time in India. After his discharge in
1892 he returned to Sowerby and worked
in Bamlett's timber yard – see p. 32. He
combined this with farm work in the
summer and a job as village lamplighter.

Bill Norris of Sowerby at threshing
time, 1880s. He is standing at the rear
of a threshing machine similar to that
on the opposite page. This is an
excellent costume study of a farm
hand.

Mrs Mary Harland of Sowerby, 1832–1909. This old lady was mother-in-law to John Norris, on the previous page. She is sitting outside her cottage in Silver Street in 1905; modern bungalows have been built there now.

Mrs Martha Sophia Plummer of Thormanby Hall, *c.* 1910. This lady, busy with crochet-hook in her garden, was born near Darlington in 1844, and came to Thormanby as the wife of farmer William Henry Plummer. She died in about 1930.

The Robinson family of Thormanby Hill, late 1920s. Dora Robinson, seen here with her husband, Joseph, and son, George, was the daughter of Mrs Plummer opposite. The family farmed at Thormanby Hill, and retired to Sowerby in the 1930s.

The Johnson sisters of Thirsk, c. 1900. This charming portrait shows the daughters of William Johnson, founder of Thirsk's noted butcher's business (p. 30). Edith, on the left, became a nurse (see p. 52), Mabel, on the right, married, becoming Mrs Shaw, while Ethel, the youngest, inherited the business and was a great benefactress to the town. Clarke's studio props also appear in the portrait of Corporal Lazenby on p. 55.

Dr and Mrs MacArthur, 1914. Dr MacArthur came to Thirsk in 1910 as junior partner to Dr Buchanan, after whose tragic early death he took over the practice, later marrying Dr Buchanan's sister. He served in the RAMC during the First World War.

Dr MacArthur was a great horseman, and regularly rode out to visit patients in outlying farms and villages. He was in his 70s when this photograph was taken in the late 1950s; the horse is one that he bred himself.

SPORT AND
ENTERTAINMENT

*Thirsk Flute Band, early 1900s. This is possibly
the successor to the 'drum and fife' band known
to have been formed by John Thomas Fox
(1840–1906), 'journalist, musician and
composer'.*

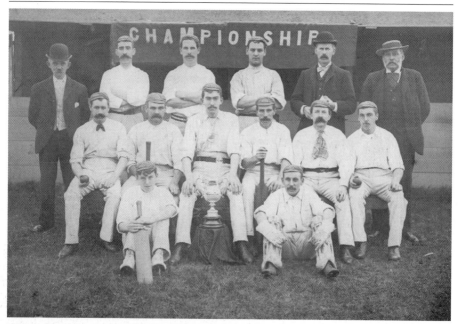

Thirsk Victoria Cricket Team, winners of the Northallerton and District League Cup, 1898. The umpires stand on either side; the tall figure in the bowler hat is the scorer.

George Freeman, Yorkshire and England 1866–72. As befits the town where Thomas Lord was born in 1755, Thirsk has produced some notable cricketers. Freeman was a formidable fast bowler, the terror of Lancashire players and a grim opponent of W.G. Grace. He topped the bowling averages in 1871, but retired at the age of 27 to devote himself to his business as cattle auctioneer.

Thirsk XI, 1908. The rakish straw hats were clearly part of club uniform. Apart from the batsman's pads, there is no other sign of protective gear. The team includes some well-known personalities. Back row, left to right: J.T. Lynch (scorer), W.J. Horner, H. Pearson, W. Barker, F.R. Hansell, R. Bolton, O. Firth, E.B. Peat, W.K. Macaulay, A. Busfield (umpire). Front row: A.B. Marsh, Z. Wright, E. Foggitt. 'Tinner' Bolton was noted for his powerful voice; legend has it that his mighty appeal for lbw on the Thirsk ground resulted in a batsman being given 'out' in a match being played at Sowerby!

Thirsk 1st XI, winners of the Senior League Cup, 1920. Back row, left to right: H. Horner, W. Boddy, F. Fawell, S. Clayton, A. Rooke, L. Ryder, M. Lister, J. Blakey. Second row: Ed. Mitchell, A. Mayne, A. Pearson, Reg. Bell, Esq., E.R. Turton, Esq., MP, A.E. Peatfield, J.H. Wright. Front row: Turp. Atkinson, J.E. Backhouse, W. Wright. Captain Reginald Bell was the squire of Thirsk; he took a keen interest in sport, but by now in his 70s, he looks bowed and frail in this photograph; he died the following year. Captain Edmund Turton was the owner of the Upsall Castle estate and MP for the district.

G.G. Macaulay, Yorkshire and England player, 1921–35. Born in 1897, the son of a Thirsk innkeeper, George Gibson Macaulay was already making a name for himself at the age of 14. In 1923 he took a wicket with his very first ball in his first Test Match and went on to play for England seven more times. Arthritis led to his premature retirement from the game in 1935; he was killed in 1940 on active service with the RAF. Neville Cardus described him as 'a grand fellow off the field, but a tiger with the temper of the jungle on it'.

Kilburn, winners of the Felixkirk and District League Cup, 1957. Revd R.J.L.E. King, Chairman, is seen presenting the cup to Kilburn captain Peter Smith. This cup was keenly contested by local teams, but in later years Kilburn won it so often that it almost became a formality!

Thirsk Football Club, 1905/6. We have no names for the members of this team, but the photograph is of interest not just for the players, but for the supporters who are displaying appropriate gear. Note in particular the large rattle on the left, once an essential item of a supporter's kit.

Husthwaite Ladies' Hockey Team, 1922. This is another photograph where the period costume details are fascinating.

Thirsk Athletic Club Hockey Team, 1926/7. Back row, left to right: G. Brown, I.A. Sleightholme, H. Bulmer, C. Pearson, M. Lister. Second row: E.R. Jackson, L. Ryder, H. Greenwood, P. Campbell. Front row: F.S. Constable, H. Walker. Ryder and Lister were also cricketers – see p. 112.

Thirsk Men's Hockey Team, 1930s. Harry Bulmer is the umpire on the left – see above and p. 55. In the centre of the front row is Alfred Rutherford, later Secretary to the Athletic Club, a leading figure in country sport and enthusiast for amateur dramatics.

Royal visit to Thirsk Races, 1895. Edward VII, then Prince of Wales, was a visitor to Thirsk in October 1895. This small stand was built for the occasion, and stood until the present grandstand was erected in 1924. There has been racing here since 1854.

Motor cycle contests on Sutton Bank, 1921. The notorious gradient here was a popular venue for motor cycle trials. This scene at the check point shows an interesting group of early side-car outfits.

Thirsk Swimming Club pool, opened 16 August 1910. The 'pool' was a deep section of the Cod Beck upstream from Norby. The primitive facilities provided are clearly shown.

Thirsk and Sowerby fishing match, 1899. The group is probably posed on the banks of the Cod Beck before the match began. The expressions of the competitors suggest that this was no light-hearted contest.

Thirsk and Sowerby Prize Silver Band, late 1920s. The band is shown at Upsall Castle, the home of its president, Sir Edmund Turton, who is seated at the centre of the front row. During the inter-war years, the band was a flourishing organization, competing regularly and successfully at band contests as far afield as Crystal Palace. During the Second World War the band's operations were suspended; once the war was over several unsuccessful attempts were made to re-form, but the band was finally wound up in 1950. Prominent in the centre of the back row is bandsman Reginald Reast, who joined the band in 1920; his brothers Clement and Sidney are sitting in the front row.

Thirsk Ragtime Band, 1911. We know little about this band, but the assortment of instruments is intriguing. *Alexander's Ragtime Band*, Irving Berlin's hit number, was written in 1911.

Thirsk Coronation Harmonica Band, 1937. When plans were made to celebrate the coronation of George VI on 12 May 1937, the Silver Band had been booked elsewhere. The Harmonica Band was formed by Albert Swift (seated at the front) to fill the gap. It was an instant success and went on to win a prize at Belle Vue, Manchester. It continued to entertain until the war.

Heralds form the prologue to the Thirsk Historical Play, June 1907. This large-scale pageant was performed in the grounds of Thirsk Hall to raise funds for insuring the parish church. Music was provided by the organist, Mr A.J. Todd, direction by Mr D'Arcy de Ferrars. Special trains were run to the event.

Norse warriors prepare to sacrifice a British maiden. Coifi, the priest of Thor (played by Revd Eusebius Richardson), had just cried: 'Again shall human sacrifice atone for all the lands on which Thor's name is set.' The maiden is saved in the nick of time by the intervention of the Christian Felix.

The Market Scene. This was a comic interlude during the play; the Constable (in black) presents two offending butchers (chained) to the Bailiff (with whip), attended by the Bellman. The incidents portrayed, however, are all to be found in the Manor Court rolls.

The Maypole Dancers. Children played a large part in many scenes; the maypole was brought on in the finale as part of the general rejoicing. The photographers did a roaring trade, and pictures of the play regularly turn up. The pageant was revived in 1933 in aid of the church school.

The Constitutional Bazaar, 1913. The Town Hall and associated Constitutional Club were newly built in 1913; this fund-raising event is taking place outside the hall. The bearded figure in the background is Revd Eusebius Richardson once again. The man with the moustache holding the left-hand side of the 'Aunt Sally' notice is Walter Power. He brought the cinema to Thirsk in 1912 when he opened the Picture House in the old Institute building. Generally known as 'Power's', it later became the Ritz, and more recently, Studio One. Power not only ran the cinema but also played the accompaniment to the silent films; he was 'a popular personality and showman extraordinary'.

Concert Party, 1917. Walter Power is seated first on the left with the other performers in a concert party organized on behalf of the soldiers at the Red Cross hospital next door to his Picture House. Mr and Mrs Power were presented with a silver cruet that year from 'the Wounded Boys' in appreciation of the entertainments he provided.

Comic dresses, Carlton Husthwaite Sports, 1926. This variation on the fancy dress competition was a popular event, and the competitors have shown ingenuity. Charlie Chaplin is represented on the left, but we can only guess at the other characters.

Sangers Circus arrives in Thirsk, 1800s. This is an early photograph and has faded, but it conveys an idea of the procession of ornate vans and carriages that marked the arrival of this famous circus on the showground (probably along Sutton Road). The running figures on the left show that the parade is still on the move.

Amateur dramatics, early 1900s. Pencilled on the back of this photograph is 'Thirsk Historical Play', but there was no eighteenth-century episode in that production. It may be a group from a musical comedy of about the same time.

Thirsk and Sowerby Amateurs, 1934. The history of this local company dates from 1931 when a fund-raising pantomime first brought talent to the fore. The 1934 performances of *Miss Hook of Holland* saw Alfred Rutherford in his first leading role. This photograph shows him centre as a bandmaster Van Vuyt. He served in the RAF during the war, but returned to work with the amateurs in their post-war shows.

The cast of *Miss Hook of Holland*, 1934. By all accounts, this was a most successful show. The young leading man was partnered by the delightfully named Blossom Smith. Sixty years on, the Amateurs are still going strong.

Acknowledgements

Our thanks are due first of all to Thirsk Museum Society for permission to make extensive use of photographs from the museum collection; they have formed the basis of our selection for this book. We are also much indebted to Mr Ray Ballard, Mr Joseph Fyles, Mrs Mary Horner, Revd Eric Norris of St Mary's and Mr Roger Todd who have made original photographs available to us or have allowed us to take copies. A number of people have provided us with information or have helped to solve puzzles raised by some of our pictures; in particular we are grateful to Mrs Annie Taylor of Carlton Husthwaite whose memories of earlier days there have been invaluable, to Mr Brian Outtrim for material on Bamlett's, and to Mr Tom Hodgson for the history of the Harmonica Band. The resources of the North Yorkshire County Record Office and of the County Library have served us well in the course of our researches. Finally, we owe a great deal to all those who over the last twenty years have deposited photographs, postcards and associated documentary material in Thirsk Museum, thus preserving for future generations an archive that grows in value as the years go by; it is thanks to them above all that we have been able to put together the volume we now present.

JCH
PHW
February 1995

BRITAIN IN OLD PHOTOGRAPHS

Scunthorpe, *D Taylor*
Skegness, *W Kime*
Around Skegness, *W Kime*

LONDON

Balham and Tooting, *P Loobey*
Crystal Palace, Penge & Anerley, *M Scott*
Greenwich and Woolwich, *K Clark*
Hackney: A Second Selection, *D Mander*
Lewisham and Deptford, *J Coulter*
Lewisham and Deptford: A Second Selection, *J Coulter*
Streatham, *P Loobey*
Around Whetstone and North Finchley, *J Heathfield*
Woolwich, *B Evans*

MONMOUTHSHIRE

Chepstow and the River Wye, *A Rainsbury*
Monmouth and the River Wye, *Monmouth Museum*

NORFOLK

Great Yarmouth, *M Teun*
Norwich, *M Colman*
Wymondham and Attleborough, *P Yaxley*

NORTHAMPTONSHIRE

Around Stony Stratford, *A Lambert*

NOTTINGHAMSHIRE

Arnold and Bestwood, *M Spick*
Arnold and Bestwood: A Second Selection, *M Spick*
Changing Face of Nottingham, *G Oldfield*
Mansfield, *Old Mansfield Society*
Around Newark, *T Warner*
Nottingham: 1944–1974, *D Whitworth*
Sherwood Forest, *D Ottewell*
Victorian Nottingham, *M Payne*

OXFORDSHIRE

Around Abingdon, *P Horn*
Banburyshire, *M Barnett & S Gosling*
Burford, *A Jewell*
Around Didcot and the Hagbournes, *B Lingham*
Garsington, *M Gunther*
Around Henley-on-Thames, *S Ellis*
Oxford: The University, *J Rhodes*
Thame to Watlington, *N Hood*
Around Wallingford, *D Beasley*
Witney, *T Worley*
Around Witney, *C Mitchell*
Witney District, *T Worley*
Around Woodstock, *J Bond*

POWYS

Brecon, *Brecknock Museum*
Welshpool, *E Bredsdorff*

SHROPSHIRE

Shrewsbury, *D Trumper*
Whitchurch to Market Drayton, *M Morris*

SOMERSET

Bath, *J Hudson*
Bridgwater and the River Parrett, *R Fitzhugh*
Bristol, *D Moorcroft & N Campbell-Sharp*
Changing Face of Keynsham,
  B Lowe & M Whitehead

Chard and Ilminster, *G Gosling & F Huddy*
Crewkerne and the Ham Stone Villages,
  G Gosling & F Huddy
Around Keynsham and Saltford, *B Lowe & T Brown*
Midsomer Norton and Radstock, *C Howell*
Somerton, Ilchester and Langport, *G Gosling & F Huddy*
Taunton, *N Chipchase*
Around Taunton, *N Chipchase*
Wells, *C Howell*
Weston-Super-Mare, *S Poole*
Around Weston-Super-Mare, *S Poole*
West Somerset Villages, *K Houghton & L Thomas*

STAFFORDSHIRE

Aldridge, *J Farrow*
Bilston, *E Rees*
Black Country Transport: Aviation, *A Brew*
Around Burton upon Trent, *G Sowerby & R Farman*
Bushbury, *A Chatwin, M Mills & E Rees*
Around Cannock, *M Mills & S Belcher*
Around Leek, *R Poole*
Lichfield, *H Clayton & K Simmons*
Around Pattingham and Wombourne, *M Griffiths,*
  P Leigh & M Mills
Around Rugeley, *T Randall & J Anslow*
Smethwick, *J Maddison*
Stafford, *J Anslow & T Randall*
Around Stafford, *J Anslow & T Randall*
Stoke-on-Trent, *I Lawley*
Around Tamworth, *R Sulima*
Around Tettenhall and Codsall, *M Mills*
Tipton, Wednesbury and Darlaston, *R Pearson*
Walsall, *D Gilbert & M Lewis*
Wednesbury, *I Bott*
West Bromwich, *R Pearson*

SUFFOLK

Ipswich: A Second Selection, *D Kindred*
Around Ipswich, *D Kindred*
Around Mildenhall, *C Dring*
Southwold to Aldeburgh, *H Phelps*
Around Woodbridge, *H Phelps*

SURREY

Cheam and Belmont, *P Berry*
Croydon, *S Bligh*
Dorking and District, *K Harding*
Around Dorking, *A Jackson*
Around Epsom, *P Berry*
Farnham: A Second Selection, *J Parratt*
Around Haslemere and Hindhead, *T Winter & G Collyer*
Richmond, *Richmond Local History Society*
Sutton, *P Berry*

SUSSEX

Arundel and the Arun Valley, *J Godfrey*
Bishopstone and Seaford, *P Pople & P Berry*
Brighton and Hove, *J Middleton*
Brighton and Hove: A Second Selection, *J Middleton*
Around Crawley, *M Goldsmith*
Hastings, *P Haines*
Hastings: A Second Selection, *P Haines*
Around Haywards Heath, *J Middleton*
Around Heathfield, *A Gillet & B Russell*
Around Heathfield: A Second Selection,
  A Gillet & B Russell
High Weald, *B Harwood*
High Weald: A Second Selection, *B Harwood*
Horsham and District, *T Wales*

Lewes, *J Middleton*
RAF Tangmere, *A Saunders*
Around Rye, *A Dickinson*
Around Worthing, *S White*

WARWICKSHIRE

Along the Avon from Stratford to Tewkesbury, *J Jeremiah*
Bedworth, *J Burton*
Coventry, *D McGrory*
Around Coventry, *D McGrory*
Nuneaton, *S Clews & S Vaughan*
Around Royal Leamington Spa, *J Cameron*
Around Royal Leamington Spa: A Second Selection,
  J Cameron
Around Warwick, *R Booth*

WESTMORLAND

Eden Valley, *J Marsh*
Kendal, *M & P Duff*
South Westmorland Villages, *J Marsh*
Westmorland Lakes, *J Marsh*

WILTSHIRE

Around Amesbury, *P Daniels*
Chippenham and Lacock, *A Wilson & M Wilson*
Around Corsham and Box, *A Wilson & M Wilson*
Around Devizes, *D Buxton*
Around Highworth, *G Tanner*
Around Highworth and Faringdon, *G Tanner*
Around Malmesbury, *A Wilson*
Marlborough: A Second Selection, *P Colman*
Around Melksham,
  Melksham and District Historical Association
Nadder Valley, *R. Sawyer*
Salisbury, *P Saunders*
Salisbury: A Second Selection, *P Daniels*
Salisbury: A Third Selection, *P Daniels*
Around Salisbury, *P Daniels*
Swindon: A Third Selection, *The Swindon Society*
Swindon: A Fourth Selection, *The Swindon Society*
Trowbridge, *M Marshman*
Around Wilton, *P Daniels*
Around Wootton Bassett, Cricklade and Purton, *T Sharp*

WORCESTERSHIRE

Evesham to Bredon, *F Archer*
Around Malvern, *K Smith*
Around Pershore, *M Dowty*
Redditch and the Needle District, *R Saunders*
Redditch: A Second Selection, *R Saunders*
Around Tenbury Wells, *D Green*
Worcester, *M Dowty*
Around Worcester, *R Jones*
Worcester in a Day, *M Dowty*
Worcestershire at Work, *R Jones*

YORKSHIRE

Huddersfield: A Second Selection, *H Wheeler*
Huddersfield: A Third Selection, *H Wheeler*
Leeds Road and Rail, *R Vickers*
Pontefract, *R van Riel*
Scarborough, *D Coggins*
Scarborough's War Years, *R Percy*
Skipton and the Dales, *Friends of the Craven Museum*
Around Skipton-in-Craven, *Friends of the Craven Museum*
Yorkshire Wolds, *I & M Sumner*